EARTH DAY

by Charly Haley

Cody Koala

An Imprint of Pop!
popbooksonline.com

abdobooks.com
Published by Pop!, a division of ABDO, PO Box 398166, Minneapolis, Minnesota 55439. Copyright © 2019 by POP, LLC. International copyrights reserved in all countries. No part of this book may be reproduced in any form without written permission from the publisher. Pop!™ is a trademark and logo of POP, LLC.

Printed in the United States of America, North Mankato, Minnesota

082018
012019

THIS BOOK CONTAINS
RECYCLED MATERIALS

Cover Photo: iStockphoto
Interior Photos: iStockphoto, 1, 5, 19 (top), 19 (bottom left), 19 (bottom right), 21; Shutterstock Images, 7, 10, 15, 16; Robert Kradin/AP Images, 9; Mark Hoffman/AP Images, 11; AP Images, 12

Editor: Meg Gaertner
Series Designer: Laura Mitchell

Library of Congress Control Number: 2018949959
Publisher's Cataloging-in-Publication Data
Names: Haley, Charly, author.
Title: Earth day / by Charly Haley.
Description: Minneapolis, Minnesota : Pop!, 2019 | Series: Holidays | Includes online resources and index.
Identifiers: ISBN 9781532161964 (lib. bdg.) | ISBN 9781641855679 (pbk) | ISBN 9781532163029 (ebook)
Subjects: LCSH: Earth day--Juvenile literature. | Holidays--Juvenile literature. | Environmental stewardship--Juvenile literature.
Classification: DDC 394.262--dc23

Hello! My name is

Cody Koala

Pop open this book and you'll find QR codes like this one, loaded with information, so you can learn even more!

Scan this code* and others like it while you read, or visit the website below to make this book pop.

popbooksonline.com/earth-day

*Scanning QR codes requires a web-enabled smart device with a QR code reader app and a camera.

Table of Contents

Chapter 1
Earth Day 4

Chapter 2
The First Earth Day 8

Chapter 3
Protecting Earth. 14

Chapter 4
Celebrations 18

Making Connections 22
Glossary. 23
Index 24
Online Resources 24

Chapter 1

Earth Day

People are planting trees.

They are picking up trash.

It is Earth Day.

Watch a video here!

Earth Day is celebrated every year on April 22. The holiday encourages people to take care of the **environment**.

April

Mon	Tue	Wed	Thu	Fri	Sat	Sun
						1
2	3	4	5	6	7	8
9	10	11	12	13	14	15
16	17	18	19	20	21	22
23	24	25	26	27	28	29
30						

The First Earth Day

Earth Day was first celebrated on April 22, 1970. The holiday was created in response to an oil spill.

Learn more here!

A company spilled oil
in California. Oil spills hurt
plants and animals.

Gaylord Nelson in 2001

Gaylord Nelson wanted people to care. He was a US senator from Wisconsin. He created the first Earth Day.

People listened to Nelson. They spoke up for the Earth. They protested against companies that cause pollution.

About 20 million people celebrated the first Earth Day.

Chapter 3

Protecting Earth

After the first Earth Day, the US government made new laws. These laws are meant to protect Earth.

Complete an activity here!

But there are still people who hurt the environment. Companies still cause pollution. Some people litter. People must work together to take care of Earth.

Chapter 4

Celebrations

Many people celebrate
Earth Day each year.
People **recycle** and pick up
trash. They want to make
Earth clean.

Learn more here!

People plant trees or flowers on Earth Day. They want Earth to be beautiful. People also spend time outside. They want to enjoy Earth.

Many cities and schools have Earth Day events.

Making Connections

Text-to-Self

Have you ever celebrated Earth Day? How would you like to celebrate it?

Text-to-Text

Have you read any other books about holidays? What did you learn?

Text-to-World

Have you seen pollution in the world? How do you think people can help keep Earth clean?

Glossary

environment – the natural world, including the land, sea, and air.

litter – to throw trash on the ground instead of in a trash can.

pollution – harmful chemicals or garbage that hurt plants, animals, and people.

protest – to publicly speak out against something.

recycle – to make trash into something that can be used.

senator – a member of the US Senate and part of the government.

Index

environment, 6, 17

laws, 14

Nelson, Gaylord, 11, 13

oil spill, 8, 10

pollution, 13, 17

protest, 13

trash, 4, 18

trees, 4, 20

Online Resources

popbooksonline.com

Thanks for reading this Cody Koala book!

Scan this code* and others like it in this book, or visit the website below to make this book pop!

popbooksonline.com/earth-day

*Scanning QR codes requires a web-enabled smart device with a QR code reader app and a camera.